Freedom
&
Peace
Through
Servant
Leadership

The Art of Transformation
for a New World

Zen Benefiel, MA, MBA, TLC, DD

Introduction

In "Freedom & Peace through Servant Leadership," I bring together my diverse professional experiences with a deep exploration of servant leadership. My work focuses on creating collaborative spaces, embracing diversity, and fostering sustainable practices, all while emphasizing the importance of empathy and open communication in achieving successful outcomes.

In addition to my role at Live and Let Live, I am the founder and manager of Be The Dream, LLC, known for being a 'possibilities coagulator.' Here, I help facilitate people, places, and things to work together better, combining personal and digital technologies, best practices, and leading processes. My broad experience in organizational development across multiple industries has led to some award-winning outcomes.

My expertise in transformational life coaching involves consulting and facilitating conversations that evolve attitudes toward taking positive action in organizational development and the world at large. Recognized as an Organizational Bricoleur and Possibilities Coagulator, my unique style and results have helped thousands through my commitment to inner and outer work, vulnerability, and willingness to grow and move forward.

Moreover, my podcast "One World in a New World" is a testament to my journey. It marks my return after a 30-year hiatus from the original "One World" TV show, peering into the depth of what keeps us afraid, angry, ignorant and immobile. The 'new world' explores inner personal development and the practical aspects of servant leadership in today's global transformation post-pandemic as we co-create a 'new normal.'

A significant moment in this journey was being introduced to the Live and Let Live Global Peace Movement by its founder, attorney Marc J. Victor, during a profound apocalyptic chat on the podcast. This interaction underscored the importance of adaptable and empathetic leadership in today's changing global landscape, especially in the wake of the global pandemic.

Now, as the Co-Director in charge of Operations for the Live and Let Live Global Peace Movement, I apply my nearly 40 years of expertise across various industries, including aerospace, construction, education, event management and community activism, to facilitate positive change and empower individuals and communities.

Contents

Introduction: A Symphony of Growth through Servant Leadership

In the symphony of leadership, the philosophy of servant leadership orchestrates a harmonious blend of purpose, empathy, growth, and impact. Throughout the proceeding chapters, we embark on a journey through the realms of holistic organizational development guided by servant leadership principles.

Each chapter illuminated a unique facet of this transformative approach, painting a vivid canvas of leadership that transcends conventional boundaries. As we reflect on the tapestry woven by these chapters, a resounding theme emerges—a commitment to nurturing authenticity, fostering connections, and propelling organizations toward remarkable growth and impact.

Chapters 1-3

The Blueprint of Servant Leadership:

Chapters 1 to 3 introduced us to the core principles of servant leadership and its profound impact on holistic organizational development. We uncovered the power of empathy, collaboration, and purpose-driven performance management. The foundation of self-awareness was laid, setting the stage for individuals and organizations to embark on a journey of introspection and growth.

Chapters 4-6

Embracing Change and Well-Being:

Chapters 4 to 6 guided us through the art of embracing change, navigating challenges with resilience, and prioritizing employee well-being. We learned that servant leaders not only adapt to change but also empower individuals to lead with authenticity, empathy, and a deep sense of well-being. This holistic approach establishes an environment where individuals flourish, even amidst the uncertainties of a dynamic world.

Chapters 7-9

Authentic Connections and Innovation:

Chapters 7 to 9 delved into the transformational impact of authentic connections, serendipitous moments, and synchronicity. Servant leaders cultivate an environment where relationships are grounded in empathy, innovation thrives through curiosity, and meaningful coincidences guide decisions. These chapters showcased that servant leadership isn't merely a managerial style; it's a philosophy that shapes a future where individuals thrive, organizations innovate, and positive impact ripples beyond organizational borders.

Chapters 10-13

Self-Awareness and Purposeful Growth:

Chapters 10 to 13 unveiled the transformative potential of self-awareness, serendipitous moments, and synchronicity. Servant leaders empower individuals to recognize their strengths, embrace vulnerability, and align their actions with their true selves.

By fostering a culture that invites serendipity and synchronicity, leaders create an environment where unexpected opportunities and meaningful connections flourish, propelling organizations toward remarkable results in-house and in the world.

Chapter 14 of "Freedom & Peace through Servant Leadership" focuses on integrating the principles of the Live and Let Live movement with holistic growth. It delves into the realms of organizational development, aligning with the movement's ethos. The chapter emphasizes the importance of empathy, open communication, and collaborative spaces in achieving successful outcomes. It advocates for sustainable practices and diversity, reflecting Zen's vision of leadership in the contemporary world, where challenges and complexities require adaptable and empathetic approaches.

The Ongoing Symphony of Servant Leadership

As we conclude this exploration, we recognize that servant leadership isn't a static concept; it's an ongoing journey of growth, introspection, and impact. Each chapter unveiled a unique facet of this multifaceted philosophy, demonstrating that servant leadership isn't confined to a single dimension.

It's a symphony—a harmonious integration of purpose, authenticity, resilience, and innovation.

Servant leadership is the catalyst for a new paradigm of leadership—one that transcends the confines of hierarchy and embraces the interconnectedness of individuals and their environments. It's an approach that invites us to lead not from a position of authority, but from a place of empathy, humility, and service.

This journey, as illuminated by the chapters preceding, holds the promise of transforming organizations, individuals, and ultimately, the world at large.

As we close this chapter, let us remember that servant leadership invites us to be architects of a future where individuals and organizations flourish, where authenticity and purpose intersect, and where positive impact extends beyond our immediate sphere.

Let us continue to explore, learn, and embody the principles of servant leadership as we embark on a journey of perpetual growth and sustainable impact.

To take it to it's logical conclusion, we have the capacity for embodying a 'perfected form, fit and function' in the world today, driven by our inner desire to live in the fulness of the consciousness that we are able to perceive.

Ancient wisdom is resurfacing now, a fuller understanding available through the discoveries of quantum theory; that we are all energy connected to infinite intelligence as Divine threads incarnate, capable of achieving greatness.

Chapter 1: The Evolution of Organizational Development: Embracing Holistic Paradigms

In a world marked by rapid technological advancements, shifting cultural values, and a renewed focus on social and environmental responsibility, the concept of organizational development has evolved beyond its traditional confines.

While the traditional models of growth emphasized the pursuit of profit and efficiency, a new paradigm has emerged—one that encompasses a more holistic approach to organizational development.

This chapter explores the transformative journey of organizational development, tracing its evolution from conventional growth models to the embrace of holistic paradigms, all within the context of servant leadership.

The Genesis of Organizational Development: Traditional Growth Models

Historically, the primary goal of organizational development was centered on financial success and market dominance. Businesses sought to increase profitability through strategies such as cost reduction, operational efficiency, and market expansion.

While these approaches delivered results in terms of bottom-line growth, they often overlooked the broader impacts of their operations. Employee well-being, community engagement, and environmental sustainability were secondary considerations, leading to a skewed perspective that failed to address the intricate interplay between business and society.

The Rise of Holistic Organizational Development: Beyond the Balance Sheet

The transition towards holistic organizational development signals a shift from profit-centric metrics to a more comprehensive approach. This approach recognizes that an organization's growth is intertwined with its impact on various stakeholders—employees, customers, communities, and the environment.

Holistic development acknowledges the intricate relationships that exist within and beyond organizational boundaries, advocating for a harmonious coexistence rather than a one-sided pursuit of growth.

The holistic paradigm acknowledges that an organization's long-term viability is directly linked to its ability to create shared value. This entails aligning business strategies with societal needs, ensuring that growth contributes positively to both economic prosperity and social well-being.

Holistic organizational development strives to create an ecosystem where organizations thrive not in isolation, but as integral parts of a larger societal fabric.

Servant Leadership as the Guiding Light: Aligning Holistic Values

In the midst of this transformative shift, servant leadership emerges as a natural fit—a philosophy that aligns perfectly with the ideals of holistic organizational development. Rooted in the belief that leadership is synonymous with service, servant leadership fosters an environment where the growth of individuals, the empowerment of employees, and the well-being of the community are paramount.

The core principles of servant leadership—empathy, active listening, humility, and a commitment to nurturing potential—resonate profoundly with the ethos of holistic development. Servant leaders view their role not as dictators, but as facilitators of growth. They create spaces where open communication thrives, ideas are valued, and a sense of shared purpose is cultivated.

By placing the well-being of their teams and the community at the forefront, servant leaders inherently align with the holistic perspective, ensuring that growth transcends financial numbers and encompasses a broader positive impact.

A Holistic Development Framework: Integrating Holistic Values

Holistic organizational development, guided by servant leadership, introduces a framework that extends beyond financial measures. It encompasses a spectrum of factors including employee engagement, diversity and inclusion, ethical practices, environmental sustainability, and community engagement. By considering these elements collectively, organizations ensure that their growth aligns with the well-being of all stakeholders, leaving a positive imprint on society.

Servant leadership serves as the connective tissue within this framework. It encourages leaders to embody qualities of empathy and compassion, making decisions that resonate with the organization's purpose and values. By fostering an environment of trust and collaboration, servant leaders empower employees to thrive, innovate, and contribute meaningfully to the organization's growth trajectory.

The Path Forward: Holistic Organizational Development through Servant Leadership

The convergence of holistic organizational development and servant leadership ushers in a new era of leadership—one that acknowledges the intrinsic interdependence between organizational success and societal well-being.

This chapter sets the stage for the exploration of servant leadership's multifaceted role in the holistic growth journey. As we delve deeper into the subsequent chapters, we will uncover how servant leadership principles empower individuals, foster collaboration, navigate change, and ultimately pave the way for organizations to flourish holistically in an interconnected world.

In the chapters that follow, we will explore how servant leadership serves as the cornerstone for navigating change, embracing diversity, nurturing employee well-being, fostering purpose-driven performance management, and envisioning a future where organizations thrive through authentic connections and sustainable impact.

As we embark on this transformative journey, we invite you to explore the intersection of servant leadership and holistic organizational development, discovering how these principles can reshape the way we lead, grow, and create meaningful change in the modern world.

Reflections

1. **Understanding Evolution**: Reflect on your current understanding of organizational development. How has this evolved over time, and how does the concept of a 'holistic paradigm' fit into this evolution?

2. **Personal Experience**: Think about an organization you have been a part of. How did its development approach align or contrast with the holistic paradigms discussed in this chapter?

3. **Challenges and Solutions**: What challenges do organizations typically face when shifting towards a holistic development approach? Can you think of any solutions or strategies that might help overcome these challenges?

4. **Holistic Impact**: Consider the broader impact of embracing a holistic paradigm in organizational development. How do you think this approach affects employees, leadership, and organizational success?

5. **Case Study Reflection**: Reflect on a case study presented in this chapter. What key lessons can be learned, and how can they be applied in real-world organizational settings?

6. **Future Perspectives**: How do you envision the future of organizational development? What role will holistic paradigms play in shaping this future?

These questions are designed to encourage deep thinking and personal engagement with the concepts discussed in Chapter 1, aiding in the understanding and application of holistic paradigms in organizational development.

Additional Resources:
Books

1. **"Servant Leadership: A Journey into the Nature of Legitimate Power and Greatness" by Robert K. Greenleaf**

   - This is the seminal work on servant leadership, where Greenleaf lays out the principles and philosophies underpinning this leadership style.

2. **"The Servant Leader: How to Build a Creative Team, Develop Great Morale, and Improve Bottom-Line Performance" by James A. Autry**

   - Autry provides practical advice on implementing servant leadership principles in various organizational settings.

3. **"The Power of Servant Leadership" by Robert K. Greenleaf and Larry C. Spears**

   - A collection of Greenleaf's essays, this book elaborates on the key concepts and applications of servant leadership.

Online Articles and Resources

1. **Greenleaf Center for Servant Leadership Website**

   - Link

   - This website is a treasure trove of resources, articles, and training materials on servant leadership.

2. **Harvard Business Review – "The Big Idea: Before You Make That Big Decision"**

   - Link

   - Articles on leadership styles, including servant leadership, providing insights into effective decision-making and organizational growth.

Videos

1. **"What is Servant Leadership?" – TED Talk by Larry C. Spears**

   - This TED Talk by Spears, a notable authority on servant leadership, provides an engaging overview of the concept.

   - Available on platforms like YouTube.

2. **"Transform Your Life with Servant Leadership" – Ken Blanchard**

- Blanchard, a renowned leadership expert, discusses how servant leadership can transform both personal and professional lives.

- Look for this talk on YouTube or leadership-focused channels.

These resources will offer in-depth insights into servant leadership, its historical context, practical applications,

Leadership Organizational Structures

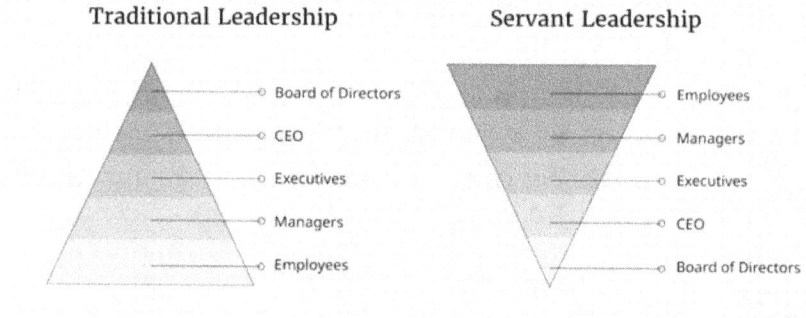

Traditional Leadership

- Board of Directors
- CEO
- Executives
- Managers
- Employees

Servant Leadership

- Employees
- Managers
- Executives
- CEO
- Board of Directors

peoplemanagingpeople.com

pe●ple, managing pe●ple

and impact on organizational culture and effectiveness. They are ideal for readers looking to deepen their understanding of the foundational principles of servant leadership as discussed in Chapter 1.

Chapter 2: A Catalyst for Holistic Growth

In the dynamic landscape of contemporary leadership, the philosophy of servant leadership has emerged as a transformative catalyst for holistic organizational development.

As we venture deeper into the exploration of this philosophy, we uncover its profound impact on fostering an environment of collaboration, empathy, and empowerment—an environment where the growth of individuals, the alignment of purpose, and the well-being of the collective take precedence over traditional notions of leadership.

This chapter delves into the core principles and practices of servant leadership and unveils its harmonious alignment with the ideals of holistic growth.

The Essence of Servant Leadership: Leading through Service

At its heart, servant leadership redefines leadership as a service to others. This paradigm shift challenges the conventional notion of leaders as authoritative figures who dictate directives. Instead, servant leaders view their role as that of facilitators, mentors, and enablers of growth.

They prioritize the needs of their teams, acknowledging that their own success is intrinsically tied to the success of those they lead. This fundamental shift in perspective sets the stage for the creation of an environment where collaboration and empowerment flourish.

Nurturing a Culture of Collaboration: Open Communication and Shared Purpose

Central to the philosophy of servant leadership is the emphasis on open communication. Servant leaders create spaces where individuals feel safe to voice their opinions, share ideas, and engage in dialogue.

By actively listening and valuing diverse perspectives, servant leaders cultivate an atmosphere of inclusivity and mutual respect. This culture of collaboration not only fuels innovation but also ensures that the organization benefits from the collective wisdom of its members.

Shared purpose is another cornerstone of servant leadership. Servant leaders work to align individual and organizational goals with a broader sense of purpose—one that transcends financial success and encompasses a positive impact on society.

By imbuing every action and decision with purpose, servant leaders inspire a collective commitment that goes beyond personal gain and elevates the well-being of all stakeholders.

Empathy and Empowerment: Fostering Individual Growth

Empathy lies at the heart of servant leadership. Servant leaders possess a keen understanding of the emotions, concerns, and aspirations of their team members. This empathetic approach not only nurtures a culture of trust but also creates a sense of belonging within the organization.

By acknowledging the holistic well-being of individuals, servant leaders create an environment where employees are valued not just as resources, but as human beings with unique talents and needs.

Empowerment is the natural outcome of this empathetic approach. Servant leaders provide their teams with the autonomy, resources, and support needed to excel. They encourage individuals to take ownership of their roles, make decisions, and contribute to the organization's growth. This empowerment unleashes untapped potential, driving innovation and fostering a sense of pride and ownership among employees.

Leading by Example: Humility and Integrity

Servant leaders lead by example, embodying qualities of humility and integrity. They are not afraid to admit their mistakes or acknowledge their limitations. This transparency creates an atmosphere where individuals feel comfortable taking calculated risks and learning from failures.

By upholding a high standard of ethical conduct and moral integrity, servant leaders set a precedent for the organization's values and contribute to a culture of accountability.

Servant Leadership and Holistic Organizational Development: A Seamless Integration

Servant leadership seamlessly aligns with the principles of holistic organizational development. Its emphasis on collaboration, shared purpose, empathy, and empowerment resonates deeply with the holistic perspective that considers the well-being of employees, communities, and the environment. In organizations guided by servant leadership, growth is not confined to financial metrics but extends to the growth of individuals, relationships, and societal impact.

As we journey further, we will explore how servant leadership forms the bedrock for navigating change, embracing diversity, nurturing employee well-being, fostering purpose-driven performance management, and envisioning a future where organizations thrive through authentic connections and sustainable impact.

The subsequent chapters will unveil the practical strategies, real-world examples, and actionable insights that illuminate the path towards holistic growth through servant leadership, creating a blueprint for leaders who seek to shape organizations that transcend conventional boundaries and embrace holistic excellence.

Reflections

1. **Understanding Servant Leadership**: Reflect on how servant leadership differs from traditional leadership models. What aspects of servant leadership stand out to you as most impactful for holistic organizational growth?

2. **Applying Core Principles**: Consider the core principles of servant leadership such as empathy,

active listening, and humility. Can you think of a situation in your professional life where applying these principles could have led to a different outcome?

3. **Personal Growth and Empowerment**: How do you see the role of empathy and empowerment in your own growth as a leader or team member? Can you identify instances where these elements were present or lacking in your work environment?

4. **Leading by Example**: Reflect on the concept of leading by example in the context of servant leadership. How can this approach influence the culture of an organization and contribute to holistic growth?

5. **Challenges in Implementation**: What challenges might arise when implementing servant leadership principles in an organization? How could these challenges be addressed?

6. **Personal Alignment with Servant Leadership**: How do your personal values align with the principles of servant leadership? Are there areas where you feel particularly strong or areas for improvement?

7. **Servant Leadership in Action**: Think of a leader you admire who embodies the qualities of servant leadership. What specific actions or behaviors make them a good example of a servant leader?

These questions are designed to encourage readers to introspect and apply the concepts of servant leadership to their own experiences and organizations, fostering a deeper understanding of how this approach can catalyze holistic growth.

Additional Resources:

Books

1. **"The World's Most Powerful Leadership Principle: How to Become a Servant Leader" by James C. Hunter**

   - This book offers a clear, practical guide to implementing servant leadership in various contexts, emphasizing its power and effectiveness.

2. **"Dare to Serve: How to Drive Superior Results by Serving Others" by Cheryl Bachelder**

   - Bachelder, a former CEO, illustrates how servant leadership can transform organizations, drawing on her experiences at Popeyes Louisiana Kitchen.

3. **"Leaders Eat Last: Why Some Teams Pull Together and Others Don't" by Simon Sinek**

   - Sinek explores the concept of servant leadership in the context of team dynamics and organizational success.

Online Articles and Resources

1. **Forbes – "The Most Successful Leaders Do 15 Things Automatically, Every Day"**

   - Link

   - This article discusses key habits and practices of successful leaders, many of which align with the principles of servant leadership.

2. **Harvard Business Review – "Why Isn't Servant Leadership More Prevalent?"**

   - Link

   - This article provides insights into the challenges and opportunities of implementing servant leadership in modern organizations.

Videos

1. **"Servant Leadership - How Serving Others Leads to Success" - Simon Sinek**

   - Sinek discusses the impactful nature of servant leadership in this insightful talk.

   - Available on platforms like YouTube.

2. **"The Paradox of Servant Leadership" - TEDx Talks**

- This TEDx Talk dives into the seeming paradoxes of servant leadership and how they play out in real-world scenarios.

- Search for this on YouTube or TEDx channels.

These resources will deepen the understanding of how servant leadership acts as a catalyst for holistic growth, offering practical advice, theoretical insights, and real-world examples of its application in various organizational settings. They complement the themes discussed in Chapter 2 and are ideal for readers looking to explore the practical aspects of servant leadership.

Chapter 3: Navigating Change – Theory U

Theory U is a change management method and a framework for transforming business, society, and self. Developed by Otto Scharmer, it emphasizes the importance of connecting to the deepest sources of self to bring about profound changes in individuals, organizations, and society.

The process of Theory U is shaped like a "U" and involves five key stages:

1. **Co-Initiating**: This stage involves building common intent and suspending past habits of judgment. It's about coming together as a group and starting to open up to new possibilities.

2. **Co-Sensing**: In this stage, participants are encouraged to see from the edges of the system. It involves going to places of most potential and observing with fresh eyes, empathizing deeply to understand how others experience the situation.

3. **Presencing**: This is a pivotal point in the U where participants connect to the deepest source of self and will. It is a moment of profound reflection, where one lets go of old identities and intentions and allows a new sense of self and purpose to emerge.

4. **Co-Creating**: Emerging from the bottom of the U, this stage is about prototyping the new in living examples to explore the future by doing. It involves

rapid cycles of thinking, doing, and reflecting to learn by doing and develop practical solutions.

5. **Co-Evolving**: The final stage focuses on institutionalizing the new practices, structures, and policies that have emerged. It's about continually updating practices based on the feedback and learning gained through the earlier stages.

Theory U is particularly relevant to servant leadership because it emphasizes deep listening, empathy, and co-creation, aligning with the core principles of servant leadership. It encourages leaders to lead from the future as it emerges, rather than just based on past experiences

In the dynamic landscape of contemporary leadership, the philosophy of servant leadership has emerged as a transformative catalyst for holistic organizational development.

As we venture deeper into the exploration of this philosophy, we uncover its profound impact on fostering an environment of collaboration, empathy, and empowerment—an environment where the growth of individuals, the alignment of purpose, and the well-being of the collective take precedence over traditional notions of leadership.

This chapter delves into the core principles and practices of servant leadership and unveils its harmonious alignment with the ideals of holistic growth.

The Essence of Servant Leadership: Leading through Service

At its heart, servant leadership redefines leadership as a service to others. This paradigm shift challenges the conventional notion of leaders as authoritative figures who dictate directives. Instead, servant leaders view their role as that of facilitators, mentors, and enablers of growth.

They prioritize the needs of their teams, acknowledging that their own success is intrinsically tied to the success of those they lead. This fundamental shift in perspective sets the stage for the creation of an environment where collaboration and empowerment flourish.

Nurturing a Culture of Collaboration: Open Communication and Shared Purpose

Central to the philosophy of servant leadership is the emphasis on open communication. Servant leaders create spaces where individuals feel safe to voice their opinions, share ideas, and engage in dialogue.

By actively listening and valuing diverse perspectives, servant leaders cultivate an atmosphere of inclusivity and mutual respect. This culture of collaboration not only fuels innovation but also ensures that the organization benefits from the collective wisdom of its members.

Shared purpose is another cornerstone of servant leadership. Servant leaders work to align individual and organizational goals with a broader sense of purpose—one that transcends financial success and encompasses a positive impact on society.

By imbuing every action and decision with purpose, servant leaders inspire a collective commitment that goes beyond personal gain and elevates the well-being of all stakeholders.

Empathy and Empowerment: Fostering Individual Growth

Empathy lies at the heart of servant leadership. Servant leaders possess a keen understanding of the emotions, concerns, and aspirations of their team members. This empathetic approach not only nurtures a culture of trust but also creates a sense of belonging within the organization.

By acknowledging the holistic well-being of individuals, servant leaders create an environment where employees are valued not just as resources, but as human beings with unique talents and needs.

Empowerment is the natural outcome of this empathetic approach. Servant leaders provide their teams with the autonomy, resources, and support needed to excel. They encourage individuals to take ownership of their roles, make decisions, and contribute to the organization's growth. This empowerment unleashes untapped potential, driving innovation and fostering a sense of pride and ownership among employees.

Leading by Example: Humility and Integrity

Servant leaders lead by example, embodying qualities of humility and integrity. They are not afraid to admit their mistakes or acknowledge their limitations. This transparency creates an atmosphere where individuals feel comfortable taking calculated risks and learning from failures.

By upholding a high standard of ethical conduct and moral integrity, servant leaders set a precedent for the organization's values and contribute to a culture of accountability.

Servant Leadership and Holistic Organizational Development: A Seamless Integration

Servant leadership seamlessly aligns with the principles of holistic organizational development. Its emphasis on collaboration, shared purpose, empathy, and empowerment resonates deeply with the holistic perspective that considers the well-being of employees, communities, and the environment. In organizations guided by servant leadership, growth is not confined to financial metrics but extends to the growth of individuals, relationships, and societal impact.

As we journey further, we will explore how servant leadership forms the bedrock for navigating change, embracing diversity, nurturing employee well-being, fostering purpose-driven performance management, and envisioning a future where organizations thrive through authentic connections and sustainable impact.

The subsequent chapters will unveil the practical strategies, real-world examples, and actionable insights that illuminate the path towards holistic growth through servant leadership, creating a blueprint for leaders who seek to shape organizations that transcend conventional boundaries and embrace holistic excellence.

Reflections:

1. **Understanding Change**: Reflect on a significant change you have experienced in your professional life. How did servant leadership principles, or a lack thereof, influence the outcome of this change?

2. **Theory U and Servant Leadership**: Consider the concepts of Theory U as they relate to servant leadership. How do these concepts complement each other in managing change within an organization?

3. **Personal Reactions to Change**: Think about your personal reaction to change. How do you typically respond, and how could a servant leadership approach alter your perspective or response to change?

4. **Empathy in Times of Change**: Empathy is a key component of servant leadership. How can empathy be effectively employed during organizational changes to support team members?

5. **Openness to New Perspectives**: Servant leadership encourages openness to new ideas and perspectives. Can you recall a situation where being open to new perspectives during a change process led to a positive outcome? If not, how could this approach have made a difference?

6. **Leadership and Vulnerability**: Servant leadership often involves showing vulnerability, especially during times of change. How does being vulnerable as a leader impact the process of navigating change?

7. **Implementing Theory U**: Think about a scenario where implementing Theory U's principles could aid in a change process. How would you apply these principles to facilitate effective change?

These questions are designed to prompt reflection on the application of servant leadership and Theory U in managing change, encouraging readers to think critically about their own experiences and leadership approaches.

Additional Resources:
Books

1. **"Leading from the Emerging Future: From Ego-System to Eco-System Economies" by Otto Scharmer and Katrin Kaufer**

   - This book provides an in-depth look at Theory U and its applications in various contexts, including leadership and organizational change.

2. **"Theory U: Leading from the Future as It Emerges" by Otto Scharmer**

   - Otto Scharmer, the creator of Theory U, elaborates on this approach to leadership and change management, making it a key resource for understanding Chapter 3.

3. **"Change Your Questions, Change Your Life: 12 Powerful Tools for Leadership, Coaching, and Life" by Marilee Adams**

   - Adams' book offers insights into how changing one's perspective and inquiry method can significantly impact leadership and change navigation.

Online Articles and Resources

1. **MIT Sloan Management Review – Articles by Otto Scharmer**

   - Link

   - Scharmer's articles on this platform often delve into Theory U and its applications in leadership and organizational change.

2. **Harvard Business Review – Various articles on change management and leadership**

   - Link

   - HBR provides a wealth of articles exploring different aspects of leadership in the context of organizational change.

Videos

1. **"Theory U - Learning from the Future as It Emerges" - Otto Scharmer**

- In this video, Scharmer explains the concepts of Theory U in a concise and understandable manner.

- Available on platforms like YouTube.

2. **"How to Lead in Times of Change" - TEDx Talks**

- These talks often feature insights from various leaders and thinkers on managing change effectively in organizations, aligning well with the themes of Chapter 3.

- Search for relevant talks on YouTube or TEDx channels.

These resources will provide a comprehensive understanding of Theory U, its integration with servant leadership, and practical approaches to managing change. They are highly relevant for readers looking to deepen their understanding of the concepts discussed here.

Chapter 4: Diversity, Inclusion, and Servant Leadership: Crafting Inclusive Excellence

In an increasingly interconnected world marked by diversity, the philosophy of servant leadership emerges as a beacon of inclusion and shared humanity.

As we delve into this chapter, we unravel how servant leadership not only acknowledges the value of diverse perspectives but actively embraces them, fostering an environment of inclusivity and crafting a tapestry of collective excellence.

This chapter explores the powerful intersection of servant leadership, diversity, and inclusion—a triad that serves as the foundation for creating organizations where every voice is heard, valued, and celebrated.

Recognizing the Power of Diversity: A New Paradigm

Traditional leadership paradigms often fall short in harnessing the true potential of diverse teams. Diversity goes beyond demographics; it encompasses unique perspectives, experiences, and ideas. Servant leadership brings a paradigm shift—recognizing diversity not as a mere checkbox but as a dynamic force that drives innovation and creativity.

By actively seeking out diverse voices, servant leaders amplify the richness of thought, enabling organizations to navigate complexities with agility and insight.

Empathy as the Bridge to Inclusion: Understanding Unique Journeys

At the core of servant leadership lies empathy—a quality that proves indispensable in the pursuit of inclusion. Servant leaders understand that fostering an inclusive environment goes beyond merely having diverse individuals present; it involves creating a space where every voice is heard and respected.

Through active listening and understanding, servant leaders bridge gaps of understanding, acknowledging the unique challenges and contributions of each individual.

Shared Purpose Amidst Diversity: A Unifying Vision

Servant leadership seamlessly aligns with the goal of fostering an inclusive culture with a shared purpose. By aligning diverse talents towards a common vision, servant leaders inspire a sense of belonging that transcends differences.

This shared purpose becomes a unifying force that enables diverse teams to collaborate harmoniously, leveraging their collective strengths to drive innovation and deliver impactful results.

Empowerment through Inclusion: Nurturing Potential

Inclusion doesn't end with representation; it extends to empowering individuals to realize their full potential. Servant leaders provide opportunities, resources, and mentorship that allow individuals from all backgrounds to excel. This empowerment fosters a culture where everyone can contribute meaningfully, building a sense of confidence and self-worth among team members.

Fostering Innovation through Cognitive Diversity: A Competitive Edge

Cognitive diversity—a range of perspectives, approaches, and thinking styles—becomes a catalyst for innovation in organizations guided by servant leadership. Servant leaders recognize that breakthroughs often emerge from the collision of diverse ideas. By creating an environment where varying viewpoints are welcomed and encouraged, servant leaders cultivate a breeding ground for creative solutions and novel approaches to challenges.

The Ripple Effect: Inclusion Beyond the Organization

Servant leadership's commitment to diversity and inclusion extends beyond the organizational borders. Organizations led by servant leaders recognize their social responsibility and actively engage with communities. Through initiatives that promote social equity, education, and inclusivity, servant leaders leave a positive impact on society at large, creating a ripple effect of change that resonates far beyond the confines of the workplace.

Holistic Excellence through Inclusion: A Fulfilling Future

Servant leadership and the values of diversity and inclusion converge to create a holistic approach to organizational development—one that thrives on the collective strengths of a diverse workforce. As we proceed through this exploration, we will uncover how servant leadership serves as a compass for navigating change, nurturing employee well-being, fostering purpose-driven performance management, and envisioning a future where organizations flourish through authentic connections and sustainable impact.

The chapters to come will illuminate the practical strategies, real-world examples, and actionable insights that guide leaders in embracing holistic growth through servant leadership. By weaving the threads of diversity and inclusion into the fabric of servant leadership, we empower leaders to create organizations that transcend traditional boundaries, celebrate individual uniqueness, and foster a culture of collective excellence.

Reflections:

1. **Understanding Diversity in Leadership**: Reflect on how servant leadership can help in embracing and leveraging diversity within an organization. How does a diverse team contribute to the strength and success of an organization?

2. **Inclusive Leadership Practices**: Think about a time when you felt included or excluded in a professional setting. How did this experience shape your view of leadership and organizational culture?

3. **Empathy and Inclusion**: Consider the role of empathy in fostering an inclusive environment. How can servant leaders use empathy to better understand and support diverse team members?

4. **Challenges to Inclusive Leadership**: What are some challenges leaders might face in creating an inclusive workplace? How can servant leadership principles help overcome these challenges?

5. **Impact of Diversity and Inclusion**: Reflect on the broader impact of diversity and inclusion initiatives. How do these efforts extend beyond the organization to influence the community and society at large?

6. **Personal Growth in Diversity**: How can your personal journey toward understanding and valuing diversity contribute to your growth as a servant leader?

7. **Actionable Steps for Inclusion**: Think about actionable steps you or your organization can take to promote diversity and inclusion. How can these steps align with the core principles of servant leadership?

These questions are designed to encourage readers to introspect and apply the concepts of diversity, inclusion, and servant leadership to their own experiences and organizations, fostering a deeper understanding and commitment to creating inclusive excellence.

Additional Resources:

Books

1. **"The Diversity Bonus: How Great Teams Pay Off in the Knowledge Economy" by Scott Page**

    - This book provides insights into how diversity contributes to better decision-making and performance in organizations, aligning well with the themes of servant leadership and inclusion.

2. **"Inclusion: Diversity, The New Workplace & The Will To Change" by Jennifer Brown**

    - Brown offers a comprehensive look at creating inclusive workplaces, a key aspect of effective servant leadership.

3. **"Blindspot: Hidden Biases of Good People" by Mahzarin R. Banaji and Anthony G. Greenwald**

    - This book delves into the unconscious biases that can impact decision-making and inclusivity, relevant to understanding diversity in a leadership context.

Online Articles and Resources

1. **Harvard Business Review – Various articles on diversity and inclusion**

    - HBR offers numerous articles that explore the challenges and benefits of diversity and inclusion in the workplace.

2. **Forbes – Articles on Servant Leadership and Diversity**

   - Forbes features insightful articles on how servant leadership can enhance diversity and inclusion initiatives.

Videos

1. **"The Power of Diversity Within Yourself" - TEDx Talk by Rebeca Hwang**

   - Hwang's talk provides a unique perspective on internal diversity and its impact on creativity and leadership.

   - Available on YouTube and TEDx channels.

2. **"How to Get Serious About Diversity and Inclusion in the Workplace" - TED Talk by Janet Stovall**

   - Stovall offers practical steps for creating a more inclusive workplace, relevant to the discussion of servant leadership in Chapter 4.

   - Look for this talk on YouTube or TED platforms.

These resources will provide a broad perspective on the importance of diversity and inclusion in the context of servant leadership, offering both theoretical insights and practical guidance relevant to the themes discussed in Chapter 4.

Chapter 5: Empowering Growth: Servant Leadership's Impact on Employee Well-Being

In the dynamic landscape of contemporary leadership, the philosophy of servant leadership has emerged as a transformative catalyst for holistic organizational development. As we venture deeper into the exploration of this philosophy, we uncover its profound impact on fostering an environment of collaboration, empathy, and empowerment—an environment where the growth of individuals, the alignment of purpose, and the well-being of the collective take precedence over traditional notions of leadership. This chapter delves into the core principles and practices of servant leadership and unveils its harmonious alignment with the ideals of holistic growth.

The Essence of Servant Leadership: Leading through Service

At its heart, servant leadership redefines leadership as a service to others. This paradigm shift challenges the conventional notion of leaders as authoritative figures who dictate directives. Instead, servant leaders view their role as that of facilitators, mentors, and enablers of growth. They prioritize the needs of their teams, acknowledging that their own success is intrinsically tied to the success of those they lead. This fundamental shift in perspective sets the stage for the creation of an environment where collaboration and empowerment flourish.

Nurturing a Culture of Collaboration: Open Communication and Shared Purpose

Central to the philosophy of servant leadership is the emphasis on open communication. Servant leaders create spaces where individuals feel safe to voice their opinions, share ideas, and engage in dialogue.

By actively listening and valuing diverse perspectives, servant leaders cultivate an atmosphere of inclusivity and mutual respect. This culture of collaboration not only fuels innovation but also ensures that the organization benefits from the collective wisdom of its members.

Shared purpose is another cornerstone of servant leadership. Servant leaders work to align individual and organizational goals with a broader sense of purpose—one that transcends financial success and encompasses a positive impact on society.

By imbuing every action and decision with purpose, servant leaders inspire a collective commitment that goes beyond personal gain and elevates the well-being of all stakeholders.

Empathy and Empowerment: Fostering Individual Growth

Empathy lies at the heart of servant leadership. Servant leaders possess a keen understanding of the emotions, concerns, and aspirations of their team members. This empathetic approach not only nurtures a culture of trust but also creates a sense of belonging within the organization. By acknowledging the holistic well-being of individuals, servant leaders create an environment where employees are valued not just as resources, but as human beings with unique talents and needs.

Empowerment is the natural outcome of this empathetic approach. Servant leaders provide their teams with the autonomy, resources, and support needed to excel. They encourage individuals to take ownership of their roles, make decisions, and contribute to the organization's growth. This empowerment unleashes untapped potential, driving innovation and fostering a sense of pride and ownership among employees.

Leading by Example: Humility and Integrity

Servant leaders lead by example, embodying qualities of humility and integrity. They are not afraid to admit their mistakes or acknowledge their limitations. This transparency creates an atmosphere where individuals feel comfortable taking calculated risks and learning from failures.

By upholding a high standard of ethical conduct and moral integrity, servant leaders set a precedent for the organization's values and contribute to a culture of accountability.

Servant Leadership and Holistic Organizational Development: A Seamless Integration

Servant leadership seamlessly aligns with the principles of holistic organizational development. Its emphasis on collaboration, shared purpose, empathy, and empowerment resonates deeply with the holistic perspective that considers the well-being of employees, communities, and the environment. In organizations guided by servant leadership, growth is not confined to financial metrics but extends to the growth of individuals, relationships, and societal impact.

As we journey further, we will explore how servant leadership forms the bedrock for navigating change, embracing diversity, nurturing employee well-being, fostering purpose-driven performance management, and envisioning a future where organizations thrive through authentic connections and sustainable impact.

The subsequent chapters will unveil the practical strategies, real-world examples, and actionable insights that illuminate the path towards holistic growth through servant leadership, creating a blueprint for leaders who seek to shape organizations that transcend conventional boundaries and embrace holistic excellence.

Reflections:

1. **Personal Reflection on Well-Being**: How have you experienced the impact of leadership styles on your well-being in the workplace? Can you recall a time when a leader's approach positively or negatively affected your job satisfaction and overall well-being?

2. **Empathy in Leadership**: Reflect on how empathy in leadership can influence employee well-being. Can you think of specific examples where

empathetic leadership made a tangible difference in an organizational setting?

3. **Fostering Growth and Empowerment**: Consider how servant leadership principles can foster individual growth and empowerment. How might this approach contrast with more traditional leadership styles you have encountered?

4. **Servant Leadership in Action**: Think about a scenario where servant leadership could have a significant impact on employee well-being. How would you apply servant leadership principles to improve the situation?

5. **Challenges to Implementing Servant Leadership**: What challenges might a leader face when trying to focus on employee well-being within an organization? How could these challenges be addressed through servant leadership?

6. **Personal Alignment with Servant Leadership**: How do your own values and leadership style align with the concept of enhancing employee well-being through servant leadership? Are there areas where you see opportunities for growth or change in your approach?

7. **Long-term Impact on Organizational Culture**: Reflect on the long-term impact that a focus on employee well-being can have on organizational culture. How does investing in the well-being of

employees contribute to the overall success of an organization?

These questions are designed to encourage introspection and application of the concepts of servant leadership and employee well-being in both personal and professional contexts. They aim to deepen understanding and inspire practical application of these principles in the workplace.

Additional Resources:
Books

1. **"The Culture Code: The Secrets of Highly Successful Groups" by Daniel Coyle**

   - Coyle's book delves into the dynamics of successful groups, emphasizing the importance of culture and leadership in fostering well-being and success.

2. **"Drive: The Surprising Truth About What Motivates Us" by Daniel H. Pink**

   - This book explores the elements of motivation, autonomy, mastery, and purpose, all relevant to understanding how servant leadership impacts employee well-being.

3. **"Lead with LUV: A Different Way to Create Real Success" by Ken Blanchard and Colleen Barrett**

- A unique take on leadership that mirrors the principles of servant leadership and its impact on employee morale and productivity.

Online Articles and Resources

1. **Harvard Business Review – Various articles on leadership and employee well-being**

   - HBR provides a wealth of articles that explore different aspects of leadership and its impact on employee well-being.

2. **Forbes – Articles on Servant Leadership and Employee Engagement**

   - Forbes features insightful articles discussing how servant leadership can enhance employee engagement and well-being.

Videos

1. **"Why Good Leaders Make You Feel Safe" - TED Talk by Simon Sinek**

   - In this talk, Sinek discusses the importance of creating a safe environment for employees, a concept central to servant leadership.

   - Available on YouTube and TED platforms.

2. **"The Happy Secret to Better Work" - TED Talk by Shawn Achor**

- Achor's talk focuses on the connection between happiness and productivity, aligning well with the themes of employee well-being in servant leadership.

- Look for this talk on YouTube or TED channels.

These resources will enhance the understanding of how servant leadership positively influences employee well-being, offering both theoretical background and practical insights relevant to the themes discussed in Chapter 5.

Chapter 6: The Art of Purpose-Driven Performance Management with Servant Leadership

In the realm of modern leadership, where empowerment and growth are paramount, the philosophy of servant leadership emerges as a guiding light in performance management.

This chapter delves into the seamless integration of servant leadership principles with purpose-driven performance management—a transformative approach that shifts the focus from mere productivity to holistic growth.

By prioritizing individual development, aligning goals with organizational purpose, and fostering a culture of continuous improvement, servant leaders create an environment where every team member thrives, contributing their best to the collective success.

Servant Leadership: A Paradigm Shift in Performance Management

Traditional performance management often revolves around numerical metrics, rankings, and evaluations. The essence of servant leadership challenges this approach, emphasizing that leaders are not just supervisors, but mentors invested in their team members' success.

Servant leaders focus on unlocking potential, nurturing growth, and encouraging self-discovery. They believe that genuine growth stems from intrinsic motivation rather than external pressure.

Purpose-Driven Performance Management: Aligning Goals with Organizational Purpose

Servant leadership finds synergy with purpose-driven performance management—a philosophy that emphasizes the alignment of individual goals with the organization's overarching purpose. When employees understand how their contributions contribute to the bigger picture, their sense of purpose and motivation soar.

Servant leaders facilitate this alignment, ensuring that each team member's objectives resonate with the organization's mission, creating a collective sense of purpose.

Continuous Improvement and Feedback: Nurturing Growth

The journey of growth is a continuous one, and servant leaders are keenly aware of this reality. They prioritize ongoing feedback and learning as integral components of performance management. Constructive feedback is delivered with empathy, focusing on growth rather than critique.

Servant leaders create a safe environment where mistakes are seen as opportunities for improvement, nurturing a culture of continuous learning and refinement.

Employee-Centric Approach: Empowering Ownership

Servant leaders empower employees to take ownership of their development. Rather than dictating solutions, they encourage individuals to identify their strengths, areas for growth, and career aspirations. This employee-centric approach instills a sense of accountability and autonomy, leading to heightened engagement and commitment.

Servant leaders provide the support and resources necessary for individuals to flourish, allowing them to contribute their unique talents to the organization's success.

Performance Management for Well-Being: Balancing Work and Life

Servant leaders recognize that holistic development extends beyond the workplace. They prioritize employee well-being, understanding that a harmonious work-life balance is essential for sustained growth.

By offering flexible work arrangements, promoting well-being initiatives, and fostering a culture of self-care, servant leaders contribute to the overall well-being of their teams, resulting in increased job satisfaction, improved mental health, and enhanced performance.

Unleashing Creativity and Innovation: A Holistic Approach

The marriage of servant leadership and purpose-driven performance management cultivates an environment that nurtures creativity and innovation. When employees are empowered, aligned with purpose, and encouraged to contribute their unique ideas, the organization benefits from a wealth of creativity.

Servant leaders encourage risk-taking, recognize contributions, and celebrate diverse perspectives, fostering an innovative culture that thrives on continuous exploration and improvement.

Conclusion: A Future of Purposeful Performance

In the chapters ahead, we will delve further into how servant leadership transforms organizational dynamics by fostering diversity, embracing change, and envisioning a future that thrives through authentic connections and sustainable impact.

Purpose-driven performance management, guided by the principles of servant leadership, emerges as a cornerstone of this transformation—a method that empowers employees, aligns goals with purpose, and creates a culture of continuous growth and improvement. As we proceed, we will uncover practical strategies, real-world examples, and actionable insights that illuminate the path towards holistic growth through servant leadership.

By nurturing purposeful performance, servant leaders create organizations that transcend traditional boundaries, celebrate individual growth, and thrive as beacons of excellence in a dynamic world.

Reflections:

1. **Reframing Performance Management**: Reflect on traditional performance management practices. How does a purpose-driven approach, guided by servant leadership, differ from these conventional methods?

2. **Aligning Individual and Organizational Goals**: Think about a time when your personal goals were aligned (or misaligned) with your organization's mission. How did this impact your performance and motivation?

3. **Feedback and Growth**: Consider the role of feedback in your professional development. How can servant leadership principles transform feedback from a critical assessment into a tool for growth and learning?

4. **Employee-Centric Approaches**: Reflect on how an employee-centric approach to performance management can empower individuals. Can you think of ways to implement this approach in your current or future leadership practices?

5. **Balancing Work and Life**: Servant leadership emphasizes the importance of work-life balance. How does maintaining this balance contribute to overall performance and job satisfaction?

6. **Creative and Innovative Environments**: Think about an environment that fosters creativity and innovation. How can servant leadership principles

help in creating and maintaining such an environment?

7. **Purpose in Performance**: Reflect on the concept of purpose-driven performance. How does understanding and connecting with the larger purpose of one's work change one's approach to performance management?

These questions are designed to stimulate thought and discussion about the integration of servant leadership principles into performance management practices, encouraging a more holistic, purpose-driven approach.

Additional Resources:
Books

1. **"Measure What Matters: How Google, Bono, and the Gates Foundation Rock the World with OKRs" by John Doerr**

   - Doerr's book explores the concept of Objectives and Key Results (OKRs), a performance management tool that aligns well with purpose-driven leadership.

2. **"Turn the Ship Around!: A True Story of Turning Followers into Leaders" by L. David Marquet**

   - This book offers insights into empowering leadership and decentralized decision-making, key elements of purpose-driven performance management.

3. **"Drive: The Surprising Truth About What Motivates Us" by Daniel H. Pink**

   - Pink discusses the intrinsic factors that motivate people, providing a framework that complements servant leadership principles in performance management.

Online Articles and Resources

1. **Harvard Business Review – Various articles on performance management and leadership**

   - HBR is a great source for in-depth articles that explore modern approaches to performance management in the context of leadership.

2. **McKinsey & Company – Insights on Leadership and Performance Management**

   - McKinsey's articles often discuss the intersection of leadership styles, like servant leadership, and their impact on performance management.

Videos

1. **"The Puzzle of Motivation" - TED Talk by Daniel H. Pink**

   - Pink's talk is particularly relevant for understanding the nuances of what truly motivates employees, crucial for purpose-driven performance management.

- Available on YouTube and TED platforms.

2. **"How Great Leaders Inspire Action" - TED Talk by Simon Sinek**

    - Sinek's talk, focusing on the 'why' behind actions, aligns with the concept of purpose-driven leadership in performance management.

    - Search for this talk on YouTube or TEDx channels.

These resources provide a comprehensive view of performance management through the lens of servant leadership, offering both theoretical insights and practical advice relevant to the themes discussed in Chapter 6.

Chapter 7: Envisioning Authentic Connections and Sustainable Impact

In an interconnected world, the philosophy of servant leadership unfolds as a powerful framework for crafting authentic connections and driving sustainable impact. As we delve into this chapter, we unveil how servant leadership fosters relationships grounded in empathy, collaboration, and shared values.

This chapter explores how these connections transcend organizational boundaries, creating a ripple effect of positive change that extends to communities, stakeholders, and beyond.

Servant Leadership: Cultivating Authentic Connections

At its core, servant leadership embraces the art of building genuine connections. Traditional leadership models often prioritize hierarchical relationships, while servant leadership emphasizes collaboration and shared growth. Servant leaders actively seek to understand their team members' needs, aspirations, and challenges.

By acknowledging the humanity in each individual, they create an atmosphere of trust and authenticity that forms the basis of profound connections.

Empathy and Trust: The Pillars of Authentic Connections

Empathy is the cornerstone of authentic connections. Servant leaders listen actively, validate emotions, and offer support without judgment. This empathetic approach creates a safe space for open dialogue, where individuals feel understood and valued.

In turn, trust flourishes, fostering an environment where team members are comfortable sharing ideas, discussing challenges, and working together towards common goals.

Collaborative Leadership: Amplifying Impact

Servant leaders understand that their role extends beyond making decisions; they are facilitators of collective action. Collaborative leadership empowers individuals to contribute their unique strengths towards shared objectives.

Servant leaders nurture an atmosphere where diverse perspectives are welcomed, ideas are exchanged freely, and solutions emerge through synergy. This collaborative approach amplifies the organization's impact by harnessing the collective wisdom and capabilities of its members.

Sustainable Impact Beyond Organizational Borders

Servant leadership's influence extends beyond the organization's immediate sphere. Guided by a sense of responsibility to society and the environment, servant leaders foster a culture of sustainable impact. They recognize that the decisions made within the organization reverberate through communities and ecosystems.

Servant leaders advocate for ethical practices, environmental consciousness, and initiatives that benefit the greater good, leaving a positive imprint on the world.

Servant Leadership and Stakeholder Engagement: A Holistic Approach

In the modern landscape, stakeholder engagement is essential for sustainable success. Servant leaders recognize the significance of maintaining strong relationships with all stakeholders—employees, customers, investors, communities, and regulators.

By prioritizing the needs and expectations of various stakeholders, servant leaders ensure that organizational decisions are informed by a holistic perspective that considers diverse interests.

Creating a Legacy of Positive Change: An Enduring Impact

Servant leaders are committed to creating a legacy of positive change that transcends their tenure. They focus on developing leaders within the organization who carry forward the principles of servant leadership.

By cultivating a culture of mentorship, empowerment, and empathy, servant leaders ensure that authentic connections and sustainable impact remain integral to the organization's DNA, fostering continuous growth and progress.

Conclusion: A Future of Authentic Leadership

In the upcoming chapters, we will delve deeper into how servant leadership shapes organizations through change, embraces diversity, nurtures employee well-being, and fosters purpose-driven performance management.

Guided by the principles of servant leadership, leaders have the opportunity to not only create authentic connections within their organizations but to extend their positive impact to communities and society at large.

As we explore practical strategies, real-world examples, and actionable insights, we uncover the path towards holistic growth through servant leadership—an approach that transforms organizations into beacons of authentic connections and sustainable impact in an interconnected world.

Reflections:

1. **Understanding Authentic Connections**: Reflect on your experiences in forming authentic connections in the workplace. How do you see the role of servant leadership in fostering these connections?

2. **Sustainable Impact in Leadership**: Consider the concept of sustainable impact in leadership. How can servant leaders ensure that their actions not only benefit their organization but also contribute

positively to the broader community and environment?

3. **Empathy in Action**: Empathy is a key component of servant leadership. Can you recall a situation where demonstrating empathy led to stronger relationships and better outcomes in your professional life?

4. **Balancing Organizational Goals with Societal Needs**: Reflect on how a servant leader might balance organizational goals with societal needs. Can you think of an example where this balance was achieved successfully?

5. **The Role of Trust**: Trust is fundamental in building authentic connections. How can servant leaders cultivate trust within their teams, and what impact does this have on the organization's success?

6. **Navigating Ethical Dilemmas**: Servant leadership often involves navigating ethical dilemmas. Reflect on a time when you faced an ethical challenge. How would a servant leadership approach have influenced your decision-making?

7. **Long-Term Vision for Impact**: Think about the long-term vision for your organization or team. How can servant leadership contribute to a sustainable and impactful future?

These questions are designed to encourage introspection and application of the concepts discussed in Chapter 7, aiding readers in exploring the depth and practical implications of authentic connections and sustainable impact within the context of servant leadership.

Additional Resources:

Books

1. **"Start with Why: How Great Leaders Inspire Everyone to Take Action" by Simon Sinek**

   - Sinek's book explores the importance of understanding the 'why' behind actions, which is crucial for creating authentic connections and a sustainable impact.

2. **"Authentic Leadership: Rediscovering the Secrets to Creating Lasting Value" by Bill George**

   - George's book delves into the concept of authentic leadership, aligning with the principles of servant leadership for sustainable and impactful leadership.

3. **"The Triple Bottom Line: How Today's Best-Run Companies Are Achieving Economic, Social and Environmental Success - and How You Can Too" by Andrew Savitz**

   - This book offers insights into achieving sustainable success, balancing economic, social, and environmental considerations.

Online Articles and Resources

1. **Harvard Business Review – Various articles on authentic leadership and sustainable business practices**

   - HBR provides a wealth of articles exploring the importance of authenticity and sustainability in leadership and business.

2. **Forbes – Articles on Creating Authentic Connections in Leadership**

   - Forbes features insightful articles on how leaders can build authentic connections and drive sustainable impacts in their organizations.

Videos

1. **"The Power of Vulnerability" - TED Talk by Brené Brown**

   - Brown's talk, which touches on vulnerability and authenticity, is essential for understanding how these qualities contribute to strong connections and leadership.

   - Available on YouTube and TED platforms.

2. **"How to Build (and Rebuild) Trust" - TED Talk by Frances Frei**

- Frei's insights on trust are crucial for building authentic relationships and creating a sustainable impact in leadership.

- Look for this talk on YouTube or TED channels.

These resources will provide a deep understanding of how servant leadership can foster authentic connections and create a sustainable impact, offering both theoretical insights and practical guidance relevant to the themes discussed in Chapter 7.

Chapter 8: Servant Leadership and Change Navigation: Embracing Transformative Journeys

In the ever-evolving landscape of leadership, the philosophy of servant leadership emerges as a guiding compass for navigating change.

This chapter unveils how servant leadership empowers organizations to embrace change as an opportunity for growth, innovation, and transformation.

By fostering a culture of adaptability, empathy, and continuous learning, servant leaders guide their teams through change with resilience and purpose.

Servant Leadership: Embracing Change as Growth

Servant leaders perceive change not as a disruption but as a catalyst for growth. Traditional leadership models may view change as a challenge to overcome, but servant leadership reframes it as an opportunity to evolve.

Servant leaders understand that growth stems from adapting to new circumstances, and they guide their teams with a positive outlook that encourages exploration and embracing the unknown.

Leading with Empathy Through Change

One of the defining characteristics of servant leadership is empathy—an attribute that shines brightly during times of change. Servant leaders recognize the emotional impact change can have on individuals.

By acknowledging fears, uncertainties, and concerns, they create an environment where team members feel supported and understood. This empathetic approach builds trust and encourages open communication, which is crucial for successful change management.

Communication as a Catalyst for Change

Effective communication is essential during times of change, and servant leaders excel in this area. They provide clear, transparent, and consistent communication that keeps team members informed and engaged.

Servant leaders actively listen to feedback, address questions, and create opportunities for dialogue. This open communication creates a sense of alignment, ensuring that everyone understands the rationale behind the change and their role in its success.

Adaptability and Continuous Learning: A Core Tenet

Servant leaders embrace adaptability as a core value. They model a willingness to learn and grow, demonstrating that change is not a one-time event but a continuous journey.

By encouraging team members to acquire new skills, explore novel approaches, and stay curious, servant leaders create an atmosphere where change is met with enthusiasm rather than resistance.

Empowerment in Change: Fostering Ownership

During times of change, servant leaders empower team members to take ownership of their roles and contributions. They create a culture where individuals feel empowered to make decisions, innovate, and contribute to the change process.

This empowerment not only improves engagement but also enables the organization to tap into the collective intelligence of its workforce, generating creative solutions and fresh perspectives.

Leading by Example: Embracing Change with Grace

Servant leaders lead by example, demonstrating their own willingness to adapt and embrace change. They model resilience, optimism, and a commitment to learning, inspiring their teams to do the same.

This approach dispels fear and uncertainty, creating an environment where change is seen as an exciting opportunity rather than a daunting challenge.

Conclusion: Navigating Change with Purpose

In the forthcoming chapters, we will delve deeper into how servant leadership transforms organizations through diversity, nurtures employee well-being, fosters purpose-driven performance management, and envisions a future that thrives through authentic connections and sustainable impact.

Guided by servant leadership, leaders can navigate change as a transformative journey, guiding their teams through uncertainty with resilience, empathy, and purpose.

As we explore practical strategies, real-world examples, and actionable insights, we uncover the path towards holistic growth through servant leadership—an approach that equips organizations to not only weather change but to emerge stronger, more innovative, and more connected on the other side.

Reflections:

1. **Perceptions of Change**: Reflect on how your perception of change has evolved over time. How does the concept of servant leadership influence your approach to navigating change in your organization?

2. **Empathy in Times of Transition**: Think about a major change or transition you have experienced in the workplace. How could empathetic leadership have impacted the process and outcome of this change?

3. **Communication as a Change Catalyst**: Consider a situation where communication played a crucial role during a change initiative. How can servant leaders use effective communication to facilitate smoother transitions?

4. **Adaptability and Continuous Learning**: Reflect on a scenario where adaptability and continuous

learning were essential. How can these elements be incorporated into servant leadership to navigate change successfully?

5. **Empowerment During Change**: How can servant leaders empower their team members during times of change? Can you think of an example where empowerment during change led to a positive outcome?

6. **Leading by Example in Change**: Servant leaders often lead by example, especially during times of change. Reflect on how leading by example can influence the team's response to change.

7. **Purpose-Driven Change Navigation**: Consider how aligning change initiatives with the organization's purpose can impact the effectiveness of these changes. How does servant leadership facilitate this alignment?

These questions are designed to prompt reflection on the role of servant leadership in effectively navigating change, emphasizing empathy, communication, adaptability, empowerment, and purpose alignment.

Additional Resources:
Books

1. **"Who Moved My Cheese?" by Spencer Johnson**

   - This classic book offers a simple yet profound approach to dealing with change, both personally and professionally, aligning well with the themes of servant leadership in change management.

2. **"Leading Change" by John P. Kotter**

   - Kotter's work is a seminal text in the field of change management, providing insights and strategies for leaders guiding their organizations through change.

3. **"Switch: How to Change Things When Change Is Hard" by Chip Heath and Dan Heath**

   - This book addresses the challenges of change and provides effective strategies for implementing change in various contexts.

Online Articles and Resources

1. **Harvard Business Review – Various articles on leadership and change management**

   - HBR is a great source for articles exploring contemporary approaches to leadership in the context of organizational change.

2. **Forbes – Articles on Navigating Change in Leadership**

   - Forbes features insightful articles on how leaders can effectively navigate and manage change within their organizations.

Videos

1. **"Leading Change: Establish a Sense of Urgency" - John Kotter**

   - In this video, Kotter discusses key aspects of leading change, particularly the need to establish a sense of urgency.

   - Available on platforms like YouTube.

2. **"How to Manage Change - TEDx Talks"**

   - Various TEDx Talks offer diverse perspectives on managing change, providing insights from different leaders and thinkers in the field.

   - Search for relevant talks on YouTube or TEDx channels.

These resources will enhance the understanding of how servant leadership can be effectively applied in change navigation, offering both theoretical background and practical insights relevant to the themes discussed in Chapter

Chapter 9: Cultivating Resilience and Well-Being Through Servant Leadership

In the modern landscape of leadership, the philosophy of servant leadership serves as a foundation for fostering resilience and well-being within organizations.

This chapter explores how servant leadership empowers individuals to navigate challenges, prioritize self-care, and achieve holistic well-being.

By emphasizing empathy, creating a supportive environment, and promoting work-life harmony, servant leaders nurture a culture where employees thrive both personally and professionally.

Servant Leadership: A Catalyst for Resilience

Servant leaders understand that resilience is a key attribute in facing the inevitable challenges of work and life. Rather than sheltering their teams from adversity, they empower individuals to develop resilience—emotional, mental, and even physical.

By encouraging individuals to learn from setbacks, adapt to change, and remain focused on their goals, servant leaders create a workforce that is better equipped to handle adversity.

Empathy as a Pillar of Well-Being

At the core of servant leadership lies empathy—a quality that is vital for promoting well-being. Servant leaders actively listen to their team members' needs, concerns, and aspirations.

This empathetic approach builds a sense of trust and connection, allowing individuals to express their emotions and seek support when needed. By acknowledging the human aspect of work, servant leaders create a safe space where well-being is prioritized.

Supportive Environment for Growth

Servant leaders recognize that personal and professional growth are intertwined with well-being. They create an environment where individuals are encouraged to pursue learning, skill development, and personal growth at their own pace.

This support extends beyond task-oriented objectives; it encompasses personal goals, passions, and interests. Servant leaders understand that fostering well-being requires nurturing the whole individual.

Promoting Work-Life Harmony

In the pursuit of well-being, work-life balance is paramount. Servant leaders champion work-life harmony, recognizing that an overburdened workforce is unlikely to thrive.

They encourage flexible work arrangements, time management strategies, and initiatives that promote a healthy balance between work responsibilities and personal life. This approach reduces burnout, enhances job satisfaction, and contributes to overall well-being.

72

Building a Culture of Self-Care

Servant leaders advocate for self-care as an integral part of well-being. They model self-care practices and promote them throughout the organization.

By encouraging breaks, relaxation techniques, and mindfulness, servant leaders create a culture where individuals take time to recharge and care for their mental, emotional, and physical health.

Strengthening Resilience through Unity

Servant leaders foster a sense of unity and support within their teams. By creating an atmosphere where individuals feel connected and valued, they enable team members to rely on each other during challenging times. This unity strengthens resilience, as individuals draw on the collective strength of the group to overcome obstacles.

Conclusion: Empowering Holistic Well-Being

In the upcoming chapters, we will delve deeper into how servant leadership transforms organizations by fostering purpose-driven performance management, embracing change, and cultivating authentic connections.

Guided by the principles of servant leadership, leaders can nurture a culture of resilience and well-being, where individuals are empowered to overcome challenges, prioritize self-care, and thrive personally and professionally.

As we explore practical strategies, real-world examples, and actionable insights, we uncover the path towards holistic growth through servant leadership—an approach that creates organizations where well-being is not just a perk but an essential foundation for success.

1. **Recognizing Resilience**: Reflect on a situation where resilience was key to overcoming a challenge in your workplace. How could a servant leadership approach have supported or enhanced this resilience?

2. **Empathy and Well-Being**: Think about the role of empathy in leadership. How does an empathetic approach by leaders contribute to the well-being and mental health of team members?

3. **Creating Supportive Environments**: Consider your current or past work environment. How could servant leadership principles be applied to create a more supportive and nurturing space for employees?

4. **Work-Life Harmony**: How do you perceive the concept of work-life harmony, and what role do you think leaders should play in promoting this balance?

5. **Self-Care Practices**: Reflect on your self-care practices. How can leaders encourage and model

self-care within their teams, and why is this important?

6. **Building a Culture of Unity and Support**: Think about the culture in your organization. How can a servant leader foster a sense of unity and mutual support among team members, especially during challenging times?

7. **Servant Leadership and Personal Well-Being**: How has your understanding of servant leadership influenced your views on personal well-being and professional growth?

These questions are designed to stimulate thought and discussion about the integration of servant leadership principles in promoting resilience and well-being in the workplace. They encourage a deeper understanding of how empathetic, supportive leadership can positively impact both individual and organizational health.

Additional Resources:
Books

1. **"Resilience: Why Things Bounce Back" by Andrew Zolli and Ann Marie Healy**

   - This book provides insights into the nature of resilience in various systems, including organizations, which aligns well with the themes of servant leadership.

2. **"Option B: Facing Adversity, Building Resilience, and Finding Joy" by Sheryl Sandberg and Adam Grant**

   - Sandberg and Grant explore resilience, particularly in the face of adversity, offering perspectives relevant to servant leadership.

3. **"The Fearless Organization: Creating Psychological Safety in the Workplace for Learning, Innovation, and Growth" by Amy C. Edmondson**

   - Edmondson's book discusses creating environments where employees feel safe to take risks, a key aspect of fostering well-being and resilience.

Online Articles and Resources

1. **Harvard Business Review – Various articles on resilience and well-being in leadership**

   - HBR offers numerous articles that explore how leadership styles, including servant leadership, influence resilience and employee well-being.

2. **Forbes – Articles on Servant Leadership and Employee Resilience**

   - Forbes features insightful articles discussing how servant leadership can enhance resilience and well-being in organizations.

Videos

1. **"Building a Psychologically Safe Workplace" - TEDx Talk by Amy Edmondson**

   - In this talk, Edmondson explores the concept of psychological safety in the workplace, crucial for resilience and well-being.

   - Available on YouTube and TEDx channels.

2. **"The Power of Vulnerability" - TED Talk by Brené Brown**

   - Brown's talk, which touches on vulnerability, courage, and resilience, aligns with the servant leadership approach to fostering well-being.

   - Look for this talk on YouTube or TED platforms.

These resources provide a comprehensive view of how servant leadership can cultivate resilience and well-being in organizational contexts, offering both theoretical insights and practical advice relevant to the themes discussed in Chapter 9.

Chapter 10: Servant Leadership and the Vision for a Thriving Future

In the evolving landscape of leadership, the philosophy of servant leadership emerges as a guiding beacon for envisioning a future of thriving organizations and empowered individuals.

This chapter delves into how servant leadership propels organizations towards sustainable success by fostering purpose, innovation, and societal impact.

By embracing servant leadership principles, leaders inspire a vision where authenticity, collaboration, and holistic growth shape a brighter and more inclusive tomorrow.

Servant Leadership: A Catalyst for Purposeful Vision

At the heart of servant leadership lies a deep commitment to purpose—a commitment that extends beyond immediate results to long-term impact.

Servant leaders understand that a compelling vision not only inspires but also guides decisions and actions.

By aligning the organization with a meaningful purpose, servant leaders empower individuals to contribute to a greater cause, igniting a sense of purpose that drives sustained motivation and engagement.

Empowering Innovation and Creativity

Servant leaders create an environment that nurtures innovation and creativity. By fostering open communication, encouraging diverse viewpoints, and empowering individuals to experiment, servant leaders enable teams to explore uncharted territories.

This culture of innovation gives rise to new solutions, products, and approaches that can drive the organization towards future success.

Authentic Leadership in an Interconnected World

Servant leaders embody authenticity—a quality that resonates in an interconnected world where transparency and trust are paramount. They lead by example, demonstrating integrity and vulnerability.

This authenticity builds trust with stakeholders and employees alike, fostering a sense of unity and shared purpose that propels the organization forward.

Cultivating Social Responsibility

Guided by servant leadership, leaders understand their role in fostering societal impact. Organizations are not isolated entities; they are integral parts of communities and ecosystems.

Servant leaders advocate for sustainable practices, social responsibility, and initiatives that contribute positively to society. By considering the well-being of all stakeholders, including the environment, servant leaders create a legacy of positive change that extends far beyond their organization's walls.

The Legacy of Servant Leadership

Servant leaders focus on cultivating leaders within their organizations who will carry forward the principles of servant leadership. This legacy ensures that the organization's commitment to purpose, empathy, and holistic growth endures.

By nurturing future generations of leaders, servant leaders shape a legacy of empowered individuals who continue to drive positive change in the organization and society at large.

Conclusion: A Future Shaped by Servant Leadership

As we conclude this exploration, we reflect on how servant leadership transforms organizations by embracing diversity, navigating change, nurturing employee well-being, and cultivating authentic connections.

Through servant leadership, leaders can envision a future where purpose, innovation, and societal impact converge to create a world of thriving organizations and empowered individuals.

By weaving practical strategies, real-world examples, and actionable insights, we've uncovered the path towards holistic growth through servant leadership—an approach that not only fosters success but also shapes a future that is compassionate, purposeful, and interconnected.

1. **Visionary Leadership**: Reflect on the concept of a 'thriving future' as presented in this chapter. How does servant leadership contribute to creating a vision for a thriving future in your organization or community?

2. **Purpose and Authenticity**: Consider how aligning with a meaningful purpose influences an organization's success. How can servant leadership help in aligning individual and organizational goals with a broader purpose?

3. **Innovation Through Servant Leadership**: Think about instances where servant leadership could inspire innovation and creativity in your team or organization. How can servant leaders cultivate an environment conducive to innovation?

4. **Societal Impact**: Reflect on the role of organizations in society. How does servant leadership extend its influence beyond organizational boundaries to make a positive societal impact?

5. **Empowering Future Leaders**: Consider the importance of cultivating future leaders. How can servant leadership principles be applied to mentor and develop the next generation of leaders in your organization?

6. **Authenticity in Leadership**: How does authenticity in leadership, a key aspect of servant leadership, contribute to building trust and unity within an organization?

7. **Navigating Challenges**: Reflect on how a servant leadership approach can help navigate organizational challenges while keeping a long-term, thriving vision in mind.

These questions are designed to encourage deep reflection and discussion about how servant leadership principles can be applied to envision and work towards a thriving future, both within organizations and in the broader community.

Additional Resources:
Books

1. **"Leaders Eat Last: Why Some Teams Pull Together and Others Don't" by Simon Sinek**

   - Sinek examines how leaders can create an environment where people feel valued and inspired, contributing to a thriving future.

2. **"The Future of Management" by Gary Hamel**

   - Hamel's book explores innovative management practices that could shape the future, relevant for leaders seeking to create thriving organizations.

3. **"Good to Great: Why Some Companies Make the Leap and Others Don't" by Jim Collins**

- Collins provides insights into what makes organizations excel over the long term, including the role of visionary leadership.

Online Articles and Resources

1. **Harvard Business Review – Various articles on visionary leadership and future trends**

    - HBR offers a wide range of articles on leadership strategies that contribute to building a sustainable and thriving future for organizations.

2. **Forbes – Articles on Leadership and Future Organizational Trends**

    - Forbes features forward-thinking articles on how leadership styles, including servant leadership, can shape the future of organizations.

Videos

1. **"How Great Leaders Inspire Action" - TED Talk by Simon Sinek**

    - Sinek discusses how leaders can inspire cooperation, trust, and change, essential for creating a vision for the future.

    - Available on YouTube and TED platforms.

2. "The Future of Work" - TEDx Talks

- Various TEDx talks offer insights into the future of work and leadership, providing perspectives on how to guide organizations towards a thriving future.

- Search for relevant talks on YouTube or TEDx channels.

These resources provide a broad perspective on the role of servant leadership in shaping the vision and direction of organizations for a thriving future, offering both theoretical insights and practical guidance relevant to the themes discussed in Chapter 10.

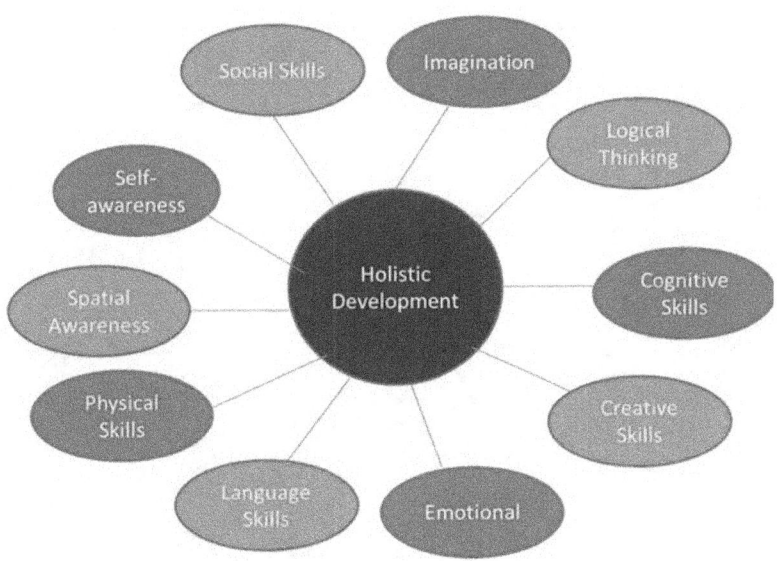

Chapter 11: Self-Awareness: The Key to Unveiling Potential

In the tapestry of servant leadership, self-awareness emerges as a crucial thread that weaves through every interaction, decision, and growth opportunity.

This chapter delves into how servant leaders cultivate self-awareness within themselves and their teams, unlocking the potential for personal and collective transformation.

By fostering introspection, empathy, and a deep understanding of strengths and weaknesses, servant leaders pave the way for individuals to thrive authentically and achieve remarkable results.

The Journey Inward: Cultivating Self-Awareness

Servant leaders embark on a journey of self-discovery, recognizing that leading others begins with knowing oneself. They engage in regular introspection, seeking to understand their values, motivations, and behaviors.

This internal exploration equips servant leaders with the clarity needed to align their actions with their true selves, serving as a model of authenticity for their teams.

Empathy and Emotional Intelligence: Mirror to Self-Awareness

Empathy, a hallmark of servant leadership, serves as a mirror that reflects self-awareness. By deeply understanding others' emotions and perspectives, servant leaders enhance their emotional intelligence and self-awareness.

This heightened sensitivity enables them to recognize their own triggers, reactions, and biases, fostering personal growth and refining their leadership approach.

Embracing Vulnerability: A Path to Authentic Leadership

Servant leaders embrace vulnerability—a powerful conduit to self-awareness. They acknowledge their imperfections and openly share their challenges and learnings.

This vulnerability creates a culture where individuals feel safe to be authentic and explore their own vulnerabilities. In this environment, self-awareness thrives, enabling personal growth and greater emotional connection among team members.

Strengths and Growth Areas: The Self-Awareness Spectrum

Self-awareness extends beyond recognizing weaknesses; it encompasses acknowledging strengths and growth areas. Servant leaders guide individuals to identify their unique talents and develop strategies to leverage them.

Simultaneously, they empower individuals to address areas of improvement, fostering an environment of continuous learning and holistic growth.

Self-Care and Well-Being: A Reflection of Self-Awareness

Servant leaders recognize that self-awareness includes attending to one's well-being. They model self-care practices and encourage individuals to prioritize their mental, emotional, and physical health.

This holistic approach not only nurtures well-being but also aligns with the tenets of self-awareness—knowing when to rest, seek support, and engage in self-reflection.

Conclusion: Self-Awareness as a Catalyst for Transformation

As we delve into the subsequent chapters, we'll continue exploring how servant leadership propels organizations towards success through serendipitous and synchronistic moments, fostering authentic connections, and embracing change.

By nurturing self-awareness within themselves and their teams, servant leaders empower individuals to grow, lead authentically, and create a culture of continuous improvement.

Through practical strategies, real-world examples, and actionable insights, we'll unveil the path towards holistic growth through servant leadership—an approach that recognizes self-awareness as the foundation for unlocking unparalleled potential.

1. **Exploring Self-Awareness**: Reflect on your journey of self-awareness. How has increased self-awareness impacted your leadership style or your role within a team?

2. **Empathy and Emotional Intelligence**: Consider how developing empathy and emotional intelligence has influenced your interactions with others. Can you identify specific instances where these skills have been beneficial?

3. **Vulnerability in Leadership**: Think about a time when showing vulnerability as a leader or team member was challenging. How did this vulnerability impact your relationships and effectiveness in your role?

4. **Recognizing Strengths and Growth Areas**: Reflect on your strengths and areas for growth. How do you balance focusing on your strengths while also addressing areas where you need improvement?

5. **Self-Care and Leadership**: How do you incorporate self-care into your leadership practice? Why is it important for leaders to model self-care?

6. **Impacts of Self-Awareness in Decision-Making**: Consider how self-awareness has affected your decision-making process. Can you provide an example where being self-aware led to a better outcome?

7. **Fostering Self-Awareness in Others**: Reflect on ways you can or have helped foster self-awareness in your team members. How does this contribute to the overall health and productivity of the team?

These questions are designed to encourage introspection and discussion about the importance of self-awareness in servant leadership, and how it impacts personal growth, team dynamics, and leadership effectiveness.

Additional Resources:

Books

1. **"Emotional Intelligence: Why It Can Matter More Than IQ" by Daniel Goleman**

   - Goleman's seminal work on emotional intelligence delves deeply into self-awareness, a key component of understanding oneself and leading effectively.

2. **"The Mindful Leader: Awakening Your Natural Management Skills Through Mindfulness Meditation" by Michael Carroll**

   - This book explores the connection between mindfulness, self-awareness, and effective leadership, aligning well with the themes of servant leadership.

3. **"Insight: The Surprising Truth About How Others See Us, How We See Ourselves, and**

**Why the Answers Matter More Than We Think"
by Tasha Eurich**

- Eurich's book provides valuable insights into self-awareness in personal and professional contexts, emphasizing its importance in leadership.

Online Articles and Resources

1. **Harvard Business Review – Various articles on self-awareness and leadership**

   - HBR offers a range of articles that explore the impact of self-awareness on leadership effectiveness and personal growth.

2. **Forbes – Articles on Self-Awareness in Leadership**

   - Forbes features articles discussing how self-awareness is a critical skill for leaders and its impact on organizational success.

Videos

1. **"The Power of Self-Awareness in Leadership" - TEDx Talks**

   - Various TEDx speakers discuss the role of self-awareness in leadership, offering insights into its benefits and how to cultivate it.

   - Available on YouTube and TEDx channels.

2. **"Why Self-Awareness Isn't Enough" - TED Talk by Tasha Eurich**

- Eurich, in her talk, delves into the nuances of self-awareness and its complexities, particularly in leadership roles.

- Look for this talk on YouTube or TED platforms.

These resources will enhance understanding of the critical role of self-awareness in unveiling leadership potential, offering both theoretical background and practical insights relevant to the themes discussed in Chapter 11.

Chapter 12: Embracing Serendipity: Inviting Unforeseen Opportunities

In the landscape of servant leadership, the embrace of serendipity becomes a catalyst for growth and innovation.

This chapter delves into how servant leaders cultivate an openness to serendipitous moments—unplanned, fortuitous encounters that spark unexpected ideas, connections, and solutions.

By fostering curiosity, adaptability, and a willingness to explore the unknown, servant leaders create an environment where serendipity thrives and propels organizations toward remarkable results.

The Power of Curiosity: Nurturing Serendipitous Moments

Servant leaders champion curiosity, recognizing that it ignites the spark of serendipity. They encourage individuals to explore uncharted territories, ask questions, and challenge conventional thinking.

This curiosity-driven approach creates an environment where unexpected connections and ideas flourish, fostering innovation and opening doors to unforeseen opportunities.

Adapting to the Unpredictable: The Dance with Serendipity

In a world of constant change, servant leaders embrace the unpredictable nature of serendipitous moments. They understand that plans may evolve and unexpected opportunities may arise.

By cultivating flexibility and adaptability within their teams, servant leaders empower individuals to pivot, capitalize on surprises, and turn challenges into triumphs.

Creating Space for Serendipity: An Environment of Exploration

Servant leaders create an environment that nurtures serendipity by allowing space for exploration and experimentation. They allocate time for team members to pursue passion projects, engage in cross-functional collaborations, and explore new ideas.

This freedom to experiment encourages unexpected encounters and breakthroughs that contribute to organizational growth.

Collaboration and Diverse Perspectives: Serendipity Magnified

Servant leaders recognize that serendipitous moments often emerge from the collision of diverse perspectives. They encourage cross-functional collaboration and celebrate the contributions of individuals from different backgrounds and disciplines.

By weaving together varied viewpoints, servant leaders amplify the potential for serendipity, fostering a culture of innovation and creative problem-solving.

Embracing the Unforeseen: A Mindset of Possibility

Servant leaders approach the unforeseen with a mindset of possibility. They perceive challenges as opportunities for serendipity to unfold.

Instead of fearing the unknown, servant leaders guide their teams to embrace it, recognizing that the unexpected can lead to breakthroughs that drive organizational success.

Conclusion: Serendipity as an Engine of Innovation

As we venture forward, we will continue exploring how servant leadership transforms organizations by nurturing employee well-being, fostering authentic connections, and navigating change.

Guided by servant leadership principles, leaders can cultivate an environment where serendipitous moments are celebrated and leveraged for innovation.

Through practical strategies, real-world examples, and actionable insights, we will uncover the path towards holistic growth through servant leadership—an approach that acknowledges serendipity as a powerful force that propels organizations toward unprecedented possibilities.

1. **Recognizing Serendipity**: Reflect on an instance in your life or career where a serendipitous event led to an unexpected opportunity. How did this event shape your perspective or path?

2. **Fostering Curiosity**: Consider how a sense of curiosity can lead to serendipitous discoveries. Can you think of ways to cultivate more curiosity in your professional or personal life?

3. **Adapting to Unpredictability**: Reflect on your response to unpredictable situations. How can embracing uncertainty lead to positive and unexpected outcomes?

4. **Creating Space for Serendipity**: Think about your current work environment. How can you or your organization create more space for exploration and serendipity?

5. **Leveraging Diverse Perspectives**: Reflect on how collaborating with people from different backgrounds or disciplines can lead to serendipitous insights and innovations.

6. **Embracing the Unforeseen**: Consider a situation where embracing the unforeseen could have led to a better outcome. How might a servant leadership approach have influenced this?

7. **Serendipity as a Leadership Tool**: How can you as a leader, or in your own sphere of influence, intentionally create conditions that foster serendipitous moments and discoveries?

These questions are intended to encourage deep reflection on the concept of serendipity as presented in the chapter, and how it can be embraced and harnessed in a leadership and organizational context.

Additional Resources:

Books

1. **"The Click Moment: Seizing Opportunity in an Unpredictable World" by Frans Johansson**

   - Johansson's book explores the role of randomness and serendipity in success, providing insights into how unexpected moments can be leveraged for positive outcomes.

2. **"Where Good Ideas Come From: The Natural History of Innovation" by Steven Johnson**

   - Johnson examines the environments and conditions that foster innovation and serendipitous discoveries, relevant for understanding how to create spaces for unforeseen opportunities.

3. **"The Power of Habit: Why We Do What We Do in Life and Business" by Charles Duhigg**

   - Duhigg's exploration of habits includes insights into how they can either hinder or facilitate openness to serendipity and new experiences.

Online Articles and Resources

1. **Harvard Business Review – Articles on Innovation and Serendipity**

   - HBR offers articles on the role of serendipity in business and personal growth, exploring how leaders can create environments conducive to serendipitous discoveries.

2. **Forbes – Articles on Embracing Chance and Opportunities**

   - Forbes features insights on how leaders and organizations can benefit from embracing unpredictability and serendipity.

Videos

1. **"The Hidden Influence of Chance in Life and in the Markets" - TED Talk by Nassim Nicholas Taleb**

   - Taleb discusses the impact of random events in various aspects of life, offering a perspective that aligns with embracing serendipity.

   - Available on YouTube and TED platforms.

2. **"Embracing Chance in Creative Work" - TEDx Talks**

- These talks feature speakers discussing how chance encounters and serendipity can lead to creative breakthroughs and opportunities.

- Search for relevant talks on YouTube or TEDx channels.

These resources provide insights into the importance of serendipity and the role it can play in leadership and organizational development, offering both theoretical background and practical advice relevant to the themes discussed in Chapter 12.

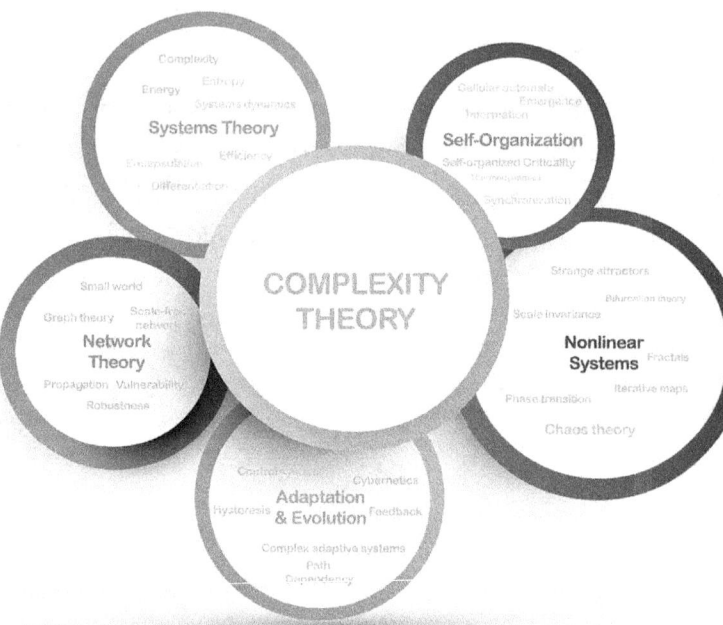

Chapter 13: Synchronistic Moments: Aligning with Universal Flow

Within the realm of servant leadership, the recognition and embrace of synchronistic moments emerge as a unique way to harness the universal flow of interconnectedness.

This chapter delves into how servant leaders attune themselves and their teams to the rhythm of synchronicity—meaningful coincidences that guide decisions, collaborations, and transformative outcomes.

By fostering mindfulness, intuition, and alignment with purpose, servant leaders create a space where synchronicity becomes a guiding force for extraordinary results.

Synchronicity Unveiled: A Dance of Meaningful Coincidences

Servant leaders perceive synchronicity as more than mere chance; it's a dance of interconnected events that carry deeper meaning.

They encourage individuals to recognize and reflect on these meaningful coincidences, viewing them as messages or signposts from the universe.

This awareness cultivates a sense of interconnectedness that shapes decisions and actions.

Mindfulness and Intuition: Opening to Synchronicity

Servant leaders foster mindfulness—a state of heightened awareness that allows individuals to recognize synchronistic moments.

Through practices like meditation, deep listening, and self-reflection, they guide their teams to attune to the present moment.

This state of mindfulness enhances intuition, enabling individuals to make decisions that are aligned with the flow of synchronicity.

Alignment with Purpose: The Nexus of Synchronicity

Synchronistic moments often align with an organization's purpose. Servant leaders guide individuals to align their actions and decisions with the organization's greater mission.

When individuals work in harmony with purpose, they create a fertile ground for synchronistic moments to unfold, propelling the organization towards its intended direction.

Creating Space for Reflection: Nurturing Synchronicity

Servant leaders create an environment that nurtures reflection and introspection. They encourage individuals to pause and contemplate their experiences, seeking patterns and connections that may reveal synchronicity at play.

By fostering a culture of introspection, servant leaders empower individuals to deepen their awareness of the interconnectedness of events.

Collaboration and Co-Creation: Amplifying Synchronicity

Synchronistic moments often manifest in collaboration and co-creation. Servant leaders emphasize teamwork and encourage individuals to collaborate across disciplines and departments.

By weaving together diverse talents and perspectives, they amplify the potential for synchronicity to flourish, leading to innovative solutions and transformative outcomes.

Conclusion: Synchronicity as a Guide to Extraordinary Results

As we continue our exploration, we'll delve into how servant leadership propels organizations towards success by embracing serendipitous and synchronistic moments, fostering authentic connections, and cultivating resilience.

By attuning themselves and their teams to the rhythm of synchronicity, leaders empower individuals to make decisions aligned with the universal flow. Through practical strategies, real-world examples, and actionable insights, we'll uncover the path towards holistic growth through servant leadership—an approach that recognizes synchronicity as a guiding force that propels organizations toward extraordinary results.

1. **Recognizing Synchronicity**: Reflect on a time when you experienced a synchronistic moment in your professional or personal life. How did this moment influence your decisions or perspective?

2. **Mindfulness in Leadership**: Consider the role of mindfulness in recognizing synchronistic events. How can you cultivate mindfulness in your leadership approach to become more attuned to these occurrences?

3. **Purpose and Alignment**: Think about how aligning with your personal or organizational purpose might open doors to synchronistic opportunities. Can you identify areas where greater alignment could be fostered?

4. **Intuition in Decision Making**: Reflect on how intuition plays a role in your decision-making process. How can servant leadership help in honing and trusting your intuition?

5. **Creating Space for Reflection**: Consider the importance of creating space for reflection in a busy work environment. How can you implement practices that allow for contemplation and recognition of synchronistic moments?

6. **Collaboration and Co-Creation**: Think about a collaborative effort you have been part of. How

might an awareness of synchronicity enhance collaboration and co-creation in team settings?

7. **Embracing the Unforeseen**: Reflect on your approach to unexpected events or challenges. How can an understanding of synchronicity change your response to the unforeseen?

These questions are designed to prompt reflection and discussion on the concept of synchronicity as presented in the chapter, encouraging readers to explore how this concept can be integrated into servant leadership and organizational practices.

Additional Resources:
Books

1. **"The 7 Habits of Highly Effective People: Powerful Lessons in Personal Change" by Stephen R. Covey**

   - Covey's book, particularly the concept of 'begin with the end in mind,' aligns with understanding and aligning with larger patterns and flows in life and business.

2. **"Synchronicity: The Inner Path of Leadership" by Joseph Jaworski**

   - Jaworski explores the role of synchronicity in leadership, offering insights into how leaders can align themselves with these moments for greater impact.

3. **"Flow: The Psychology of Optimal Experience" by Mihaly Csikszentmihalyi**

   - This book delves into the concept of 'flow,' a state of heightened focus and immersion in activities, which is closely related to experiencing synchronistic moments.

Online Articles and Resources

1. **Harvard Business Review – Articles on Intuition and Decision Making**

   - HBR provides articles that explore the role of intuition and 'flow' in leadership and decision-making, relevant to understanding synchronistic moments.

2. **Forbes – Articles on Leadership and Intuition**

   - Forbes features insights on how leaders can tap into their intuition and align with broader patterns and trends.

Videos

1. **"The Power of Intuition and Its Role in Leadership" - TEDx Talks**

   - Various TEDx speakers discuss the importance of intuition in leadership, offering perspectives on recognizing and aligning with synchronistic moments.

   - Available on YouTube and TEDx channels.

2. **"Flow, the Secret to Happiness" - TED Talk by Mihaly Csikszentmihalyi**

- Csikszentmihalyi explains the concept of flow and how it contributes to happiness and productivity, relevant to understanding synchronicity in leadership.

- Look for this talk on YouTube or TED platforms.

These resources offer insights into the concepts of synchronicity, flow, and intuition, providing both theoretical understanding and practical applications relevant to the themes discussed in Chapter 13.

Chapter 14: Embracing Holistic Growth in the Realm of the Live and Let Live Movement

Introduction

As we reach the culmination of our journey through "Navigating Holistic Growth," we venture into a harmonious blend of personal development with the practical peace philosophy of the Live and Let Live Movement (3LM), with potential for political activity. This chapter will elucidate how the principles of holistic growth and servant leadership align with the core tenets of 3LM - a philosophy that champions the rights to live freely and allow others the same liberty.

Core Philosophy of 3LM

The Live and Let Live Movement is founded upon two pivotal principles: 'Live' - emphasizing individual freedom and self-ownership, and 'Let Live' - advocating for the respect of others' peaceful existence. These principles transcend mere political ideologies, representing a comprehensive way of life that fosters personal and societal evolution.

Synthesis with Servant Leadership

Servant Leadership and 'Live' Principle: Servant leadership, which focuses on the growth and well-being of people and communities, aligns with the 'Live' principle of 3LM. It's about leading by example, prioritizing personal growth, and encouraging others to do the same. This leadership style emphasizes autonomy and self-ownership, crucial elements of the 'Live' principle.

We will briefly explore some examples and opportunities for you, as a leader, to engage. Then we will further unpack the aspects of the Live and Let Live Philosophy and how it is applied. It's simplicity is elegant.

Empowering Others through 'Let Live': Servant leadership involves empowering others, resonating with the 'Let Live' principle. It's about respecting and uplifting the rights and abilities of others, facilitating an environment where everyone can thrive. This approach aligns with the ethos of non-aggression and mutual respect advocated by 3LM.

Community Building and Societal Impact: Integrating servant leadership within the framework of 3LM enhances community and societal development. It encourages a leadership style that is compassionate, empathic, and focused on the collective good, aligning with the holistic growth philosophy.

Case Studies in Servant Leadership: Highlighting real-world examples of servant leaders who have embraced 3LM principles can illustrate the practical application of these concepts. For example, a business leader who prioritizes employee well-being and autonomy demonstrates the 'Live' principle, while a community leader who fosters inclusive and respectful environments embodies the 'Let Live' principle.

Challenges in Combining Philosophies: With cohorts, peers and others, discuss the challenges in merging servant leadership with 3LM, such as balancing individual freedom with collective responsibility. Strategies will emerge, through discussion, for leaders to navigate these challenges while staying true to both philosophies.

Call to Action for Leaders

The integration of servant leadership with the Live and Let Live philosophy offers a powerful framework for personal and societal growth. Leaders are encouraged to adopt this combined approach, fostering environments where individuals are free to grow and contribute to the greater good.

Additional Resources on Servant Leadership and 3LM

- "Servant Leadership: A Journey into the Nature of Legitimate Power and Greatness" by Robert K. Greenleaf

- "The Servant Leader: How to Build a Creative Team, Develop Great Morale, and Improve Bottom-Line Performance" by James A. Autry

These resources offer further insights into the practical application of servant leadership within the context of the Live and Let Live philosophy, providing leaders with tools to foster holistic growth in their communities and organizations.

Application of 'Live' Principle in Holistic Growth

The 'Live' principle resonates deeply with holistic growth. It encourages us to embrace self-ownership and personal responsibility, elements that are essential for true personal development. By living authentically and pursuing our unique paths of growth, we embody the essence of the 'Live' principle. This pursuit is not just about achieving personal goals but also about respecting our intrinsic freedom to choose our life's direction.

Application of 'Let Live' Principle in Holistic Growth

In parallel, the 'Let Live' principle aligns seamlessly with holistic growth, as it underscores the importance of empathy, tolerance, and non-aggression. By acknowledging and respecting the rights and choices of others, we foster an environment conducive to collective growth. This principle teaches us that our journey towards self-improvement should harmonize with the rights of others, creating a balanced and peaceful coexistence.

Integrating 3LM in Community and Societal Development

The synergy of holistic growth and 3LM principles has profound implications for community and societal development. When individuals embrace holistic growth, they contribute to a more peaceful, understanding, and prosperous society. This integration facilitates a communal environment where individual growth and societal progress are mutually reinforcing.

Case Studies and Real-World Examples

Several case studies exemplify the successful integration of holistic growth within the 3LM framework. For instance, community initiatives that prioritize personal development alongside respecting individual freedoms have led to more harmonious and productive societies. These real-world examples serve as beacons, illuminating the path for others to follow.

Challenges and Overcoming Them

Embracing holistic growth within the 3LM philosophy is not without challenges. Societal norms, personal biases, and existing political structures can often impede this integration. However, by remaining steadfast in our principles and adapting our strategies to overcome these hurdles, we can ensure that the ideals of holistic growth and the ethos of 3LM thrive in our societies.

Conclusion and Call to Action

In conclusion, the journey of holistic growth, when navigated through the lens of the Live and Let Live Movement, offers a transformative path for individuals and societies. We encourage our readers to actively apply these principles in their lives, fostering an environment where personal growth and freedom coexist in harmony.

Resources and Further Reading

For those interested in delving deeper into the principles of 3LM and holistic growth, a list of resources and further readings is provided at the end of this chapter. These resources offer a wealth of knowledge for continued exploration and understanding.

With this, "Navigating Holistic Growth" invites you to embark on a transformative journey, intertwining the principles of personal development with the ethos of the Live and Let Live Movement, paving the way for a balanced and fulfilling life.

For further reading on topics related to holistic growth and the principles of the Live and Let Live Movement, consider the following resources:

1. **"The Art of Non-Conformity" by Chris Guillebeau**: This book challenges the traditional path and encourages readers to live life on their own terms, which aligns with the 'Live' principle of 3LM.

2. **"The 7 Habits of Highly Effective People" by Stephen R. Covey**: Covey's classic book offers insights into personal and professional effectiveness, echoing aspects of holistic growth.

3. **"Dare to Lead: Brave Work. Tough Conversations. Whole Hearts." by Brené Brown**: Brown's work on leadership and vulnerability ties into holistic growth by encouraging authenticity and emotional intelligence.

4. **"Meditations" by Marcus Aurelius**: This ancient text provides philosophical insights that resonate with the self-awareness and personal responsibility aspects of holistic growth.

5. **"Nonviolent Communication: A Language of Life" by Marshall B. Rosenberg**: This book teaches communication skills that foster respect, attentiveness, and empathy, reflecting the 'Let Live' principle.

6. **"The Power of Now: A Guide to Spiritual Enlightenment" by Eckhart Tolle**: Tolle's book focuses on living in the present moment, which is a key aspect of personal growth and mindfulness.

7. **"Man's Search for Meaning" by Viktor E. Frankl**: Frankl's exploration of finding purpose and meaning in life's challenges aligns with the principles of holistic growth.

8. **"How to Win Friends and Influence People" by Dale Carnegie**: This classic on interpersonal relationships and communication skills is essential for understanding and practicing the 'Let Live' principle.

These books offer a range of perspectives and insights that can enhance your understanding of holistic growth within the framework of the Live and Let Live Movement.

For more about the Live and Let Live Movement...

LiveandLetLive.org

About the Author:

Zen Benefiel is a visionary _author_ and _coach_, adept in the realms of personal, professional, and organizational development. He is the Operations Director for the Live and Let Live Foundation and Movement.

Zen's passion lies in uncovering buried knowledge in others, a mission he fearlessly embraces through hosting transformative "_One World in a New World_" apocalyptic chats.

With a unique blend of ancient wisdom and contemporary insights, he empowers individuals to unlock their true potential and foster profound self-discovery.

Zen's work reverberates with the interconnectedness of all beings, inspiring readers to embrace mindfulness and create a harmonious, enlightened existence.

Connect with Zen:

LinkedIn: _https://linkedin.com/in/zenbenefiel_

Coaching Website: _https://BeTheDream.com_

Amazon: _https://amazon.com/author/zendor_

www.ingramcontent.com/pod-product-compliance
Lightning Source LLC
Chambersburg PA
CBHW071049290526
45795CB00004B/1399